D0300676

MEDIA

RESERVOIRS OF DOGMA

EDITED BY
RICHARD COLLINS AND JAMES PURNELL

ACKNOWLEDGEMENTS

IPPR gratefully acknowledges the support of Channel Four Television, who generously sponsored the seminar for which these papers were prepared.

IPPR would like to thank 3Com for helping to fund publications of this series of discussion papers produced by the IPPR Media and Communications Programme.

The programme also gratefully acknowledges the support of BT, the Cable Communications Association, Granada-LWT, Mercury Communications, News International and Pearson.

Z
657
R47

CONTENTS

CONTRIBUTORS

Richard Collins is Research Director of the IPPR's Media and Communication Project and a Lecturer in Communications at the London School of Economics.

Michael Grade is Chief Executive of Channel 4 Television.

Erica Jong is a poet, essayist and novelist. Her books include *Fear of Flying* and *Fear of Fifty*.

James Purnell was a researcher with the IPPR's Media and Communication Project until joining the BBC as a Senior Advisor, UK Policy Development.

Clare Short is the Labour MP for Birmingham Ladywood. She was Shadow Minister for Women until October 1995 when she became Shadow Secretary of State for Transport.

Chris Smith is the Labour MP for Islington South and Finsbury. He was Shadow Secretary of State for Heritage and became Shadow Secretary for Social Security in October 1995.

Bernard Williams is White's Professor of Moral Philosophy at the University of Oxford. He was a Member of the Commission on Social Justice (1993–94) and Chairman of the Committee on Obscenity and Film Censorship (1977–79).

INTRODUCTION

Richard Collins and James Purnell

The title for this selection of papers from IPPR's seminar on Expression and Censorship, held in June 1995, was coined by one of the speakers, Graham Murdock. Murdock reviewed academic research findings for the seminar and reached the melancholy conclusion that "there is no comfort in the studies that have been done". That is, academic studies provide no authoritative answer to the most frequently asked question about the media: "What effect do they have?" Thus, policy makers have little solid ground on which to stand when controlling media content. Yet, the strength of public concern, and the possible damage if a firm connection between representation and behaviour were established means that censorship cannot be dismissed as a fatuous illiberal prejudice. Murdock's witty play on the film title, *Reservoir Dogs*, a film notorious for its representation of violence, testifies to the strength of feelings about censorship; to the difficulties of demonstrating the effects, if effects there be, of representation (whether of violence, sexual behaviour or sexual difference) on behaviour and belief; and the pervasiveness of basic misunderstandings and misapprehensions in this domain. Murdock neatly characterised established public presumptions by citing a cartoon showing two children watching the credits of *Reservoir Dogs* on television, and the little boy saying to the little girl "Let's go out and drown some puppies!"

Long-standing concern, reaching back to the earliest days of the mass media, about possible harmful effects of representation has sharpened in recent times. Contemporary concerns about the status and role of women, supposed increases in violent behaviour and in tolerance of violence, the role of new technologies of representation and communication have all played a part, and have been highlighted by horrible cases such as the abduction, murder, and possible sexual abuse, of a child, Jamie Bulger, by other children. In spite of the lack of evidence that the killers of Jamie Bulger had been exposed to, let alone influenced by, representations of child abuse and violence to children, his death provoked widespread alarm and demands for stronger censorship of expression. Concurrently, strongly libertarian and permissive currents of opinion have argued against both censorship and the conduct of censorship bodies in the UK.

Freedom of expression in the United Kingdom may be lawfully restricted under common law (notably the laws of confidentiality and defamation) and the provisions of numerous statutes which include:

Obscene Publications Act 1959 and 1964

Contempt of Court Act 1981 (revelation of sources)

Police and Criminal Evidence Act 1984 (revelation of sources)

Video Recordings Act 1984 (video classification)

Public Order Act 1986, formerly the Race Relations Acts of 1965 and 1976, (incitement to racial hatred)

Malicious Communications Act 1988 (material distributed by mail)

Official Secrets Act 1989

Prevention of Terrorism (Temporary Provisions) Act 1989 (revelation of sources)

Broadcasting Act 1990 (especially Section 10)

Football (Offences) Act 1991 (indecent or racist chants)

Criminal Justice and Public Order Act 1994 (right to assemble, video classification)

IPPR's seminar heard papers from Erica Jong, Bernard Williams, Graham Murdock (Reader in the Department of Social Sciences Loughborough University), Clare Short MP, Michael Grade, Chris Smith MP and Frank Panford (Barrister and former member of the British Board of Film Classification). The speakers' contributions stimulated lively discussion both from the floor and the platform. We regret that we are unable to publish Graham Murdock's and Frank Panford's papers here, but have drawn on their contributions in writing this introduction.

"I am against censorship", said Erica Jong, "I prefer the chaos of uncontrollable communication." The central argument in her libertarian call for freedom of expression – "The urge towards obscenity is nothing more or less than the urge toward freedom" – and her critique of censorship is that artistic development requires freedom of expression: "Without farts there are no flowers. Without pricks there are no poems".

Moreover, because artistic development is dependent on experiment and some experiments necessarily fail, using artistic excellence as the criterion to judge whether works which otherwise would be censored should be published will chill creativity. Jong's affirmation that transgression, whether aesthetic or erotic is central to art echoes the definition of Poet Laureate Ted Hughes, that "The progress of any writer is marked by those moments when he manages to outwit his own inner police system". Sentiments confirmed in Wendy Cope's irresistible guying of Hughes' sententiousness:

> It's enough to make a copper turn to booze
>
> (turn to booze)
>
> Patrolling the unconscious of Ted Hughes.

As Jong claims, and Cope's merciless parody suggests, "Niceness is the enemy of art".

But, however widely used in everyday speech, censorship, as Bernard Williams reminded us, is sometimes an unhelpful term. Better, he argued, to refer to suppression and restriction rather than censorship. Suppression means action to inhibit ownership or distribution of material; restriction means permitting ownership and distribution but only subject to restrictions on, for example, the place where an item can be bought, the time at which it can be shown or the age range of consumers lawfully able to acquire and use the material in question.

Williams' distinction was made by the Committee on Obscenity and Film Censorship which he chaired and which was appointed by a Labour Government in 1977 but which reported, in 1979, to a Conservative Government.[1] The Committee's recommendations were grounded in distinctions, which have stood the tests of time, changing technology and attitudes. It proposed that:

> anything existing entirely in the printed word would be neither suppressed nor restricted for reasons concerned with pornography.
>
> a small class of works could actually be suppressed... where there was a presumption that a crime was committed in the course of making it.

> matter should be restricted which, not consisting of the written word, is such that its unrestricted availability is offensive to reasonable people by reason of the manner in which it portrays, deals with or relates to violence, cruelty or horror, or sexual, faecal or urinary functions or genital organs.

Albeit in what Williams himself described as "not very lovely prose", the Committee made two useful distinctions. First, between written and other representations and, second, between that which offends "reasonable people" and that which may offend but which does not offend the reasonable. They make clear that the criterion for suppression or restriction is not that of the most easily offended. They presume in favour of free speech, only allowing suppression where criminal harm is associated with the works' production. These distinctions do not solve all problems but provide a helpful basis for making policy. But they also recognise that the concern of many not to be offended by involuntary consumption of offensive representations (or, as Frank Panford put it, not to have genitalia stuffed down their throats) is legitimate. Here, the Williams Committee seems to go with the warp of public .opinion. ICSTIS (the Independent Committee for the Supervision of Standards of Telephone Information Services) found that there were fewer objections to the existence and content of telephone sex chat services, exposure to which was voluntary and by a self-selecting public, than to advertisements for the services in "family" newspapers.

Behind debates on free speech and censorship there are two main theoretical outlooks: those based on rights and those based on consequences. Behind the slogan "Pornography is the theory, rape is the practice" is an appeal to consequences; behind the slogan "Free Speech and Freedom of Information" is an appeal to rights. In practice these theoretical perspectives are not so neatly opposed. Consequentialism can be used to defend free speech, for example, as Erica Jong did in arguing that without free speech there is no great art. And rights theories can be used to defend censorship as has Catherine Itzin in arguing for censorship of pornography because it infringes women's rights.[2]

In practice, of course, most people refer to both theories simultaneously and neither rights nor consequences can be neglected. As we can see if we examine the dangers of adopting one exclusively. A rights absolutist would not override the right to free speech, however certain and harmful the consequences: she or he would defend the right to shout "Fire" in a crowded theatre which is not on fire. And consequentialism logically entails the prediction of consequences so that material giving rise to intolerable consequences could be identified. The difficulties of predicting the future should need no emphasis! Nor would the implementation of a consequentialist policy be free of difficulty for, if done democratically, the decisions of the majority could override the interests and rights of minorities. The dangers of rights absolutism are balanced by the perils of absolute consequentialism.

Accordingly, we find, even in definitions of rights, consequentialist exceptions and abridgements of untrammelled rights. See, for example, the European Convention on Human Rights where the right to free speech is limited by wide-ranging consequentialist exceptions. Article 10(2) of the Convention states:

> The exercise of [the right to free speech], since it carries with it duties and responsibilities, may be subject to such formalities, conditions and restrictions or penalties as are prescribed by law and are necessary in a democratic society, in the interests of national security, territorial integrity or public safety, for the protection of disorder or crime, for the protection of health and morals, for the protection of the reputation or rights of others, for preventing the disclosure of information received in confidence, or for maintaining the authority and impartiality of the judiciary.

The Convention makes clear that any derogations must be both "necessary" and provided for in law. However, these "consequentialist" checks on a system of pure rights are not just numerous, they could also legitimise the censorship of opinions, without requiring that there be actual or reasonably anticipated harm.

The basic principle underlying the attitudes of both the public and the Williams Committee seems to be to restrict material that causes offence, but not to suppress it without clear evidence of harm being done. However, almost anything will offend someone. How do we decide what it is reasonable to restrict and who is to decide? Where are the boundaries between the public and the private to be drawn? Is suppression and restriction to be done using the yardstick of the most easily offended? Surely not. Moreover, some suggest that action taken in response to such concerns risks masking and misrecognising more important, and perhaps even less tractable, problems.

Graham Murdock argued, for example, that demand for representation of the subjugation and humiliation of women may be a symptom of destabilising social change. Change which erodes established identity-sustaining routines, such as secure unskilled waged labour, may lead men to seek a repertoire of symbols and behaviour to sustain their masculinity through actual or symbolic violence against women. Thus, if this is to be believed, to suppress representations of female subordination is to act against a symptom rather than a cause. There is an important general truth in this specific contention. Claims of rights, and denial of others' rights, tend to take place when a lack of equity is perceived. If I am confident of fair treatment and of my own position in society, I am more likely to tolerate speech criticising me and less likely to seek out the symbolic or actual victimisation of others.

Clare Short's argument for an extension of restrictions on publication (not as she was at pains to make clear the suppression of publication) was no less eloquent than Erica Jong's libertarian appeal. Short's proposals did not (as Erica Jong had supposed) assert "that pictures of naked women in tabloids are to blame for women's unhappiness in love and inequity in finances" but testified on behalf of a "powerful, passionate, moving voice" of female protest against pornographic images of women in newspapers. Her subsequent experience of British investigative reporting, occasioned by her advocacy of the extension of the Indecent Displays Act to newspapers, made her arguments for a firmer definition of the private domain even more compelling. Short's argument was echoed by Chris Smith. Together they built a powerful argument that privacy is both an entitlement to preserve the confidentiality of personal beliefs and experiences and an entitlement to keep the personal domain free from unwanted intrusion.

Implementation of Jong's libertarian doctrine presents few problems. But if the arguments made by Short, Smith and Williams for at least some restriction and suppression have force then the questions "Who decides?" and "How do they decide?" obviously and irresistibly arise. Michael Grade testified from bitter personal experience to the difficulties broadcasters experienced under the UK's regime of broadcasting regulation. Not only were there a multitude of regulators but regulators with overlapping and contradictory mandates. IPPR research[3] on media content regulation showed that there were ten media content regulators and that the 89 members of these bodies who acted as "gatekeepers", restricting or suppressing material, were neither accountable to those who consumed and used the media – viewers, listeners and readers – nor representative of them. 57 per cent were male, only 4 of the 89 were non-white, most lived in London and were both older (the average age of the bodies' chairs was 63) and better educated (25 per cent at Oxbridge) than the population as a whole.

Frank Panford gave vivid testimony to the perils of unaccountable and unrepresentative regulators referring to what he called the "antics" of the Chief Executive of the British Board of Film Classification, James Ferman, who made redundant the Board's examining staff. Panford argued that the standards applied by regulators should be open and explicitly articulated by Parliament and that "Censors should simply be charged with the responsibility for applying these standards to individual cases". In contemporary circumstances the private decision making of the regulators ensures that the principles advanced by Jeremy Bentham of "publicity as the very soul of justice and the surest guard against impropriety" go by default. Public process enhances public knowledge and appreciation of the workings of the system, whereas a secret process by contrast keeps officials free from informed and therefore effective criticisms by those whose decisions are affected by it. Moreover, Panford claimed, now "those minded to challenge decisions are robbed of any effective means to do so because they simply don't have access to the reasoning processes employed to reach decisions". He argued that regulation must be based on principles of "legality, of openness and accountability".

Navigation between the rival claims of rights and consequences, when consequences are uncertain and rights contested, is clearly difficult and liberal democracies strike the balance between censorship and freedom of expression in different ways. Some are more tolerant of representations of sensitive matters, whether sensitivity focuses on violent or erotic behaviour, the prestige and reputation of public or private personalities, or the security of the state itself. Speakers at the IPPR seminar chiefly addressed issues of representation of sexual behaviour and difference and of violent behaviour. They came to no confident or comfortable agreement either on what should be suppressed or restricted or on who should implement restriction and suppression and how they should be performed. However their interrogation and exposition of the issues have helped the editors to draft the recommendations on content regulation to be included in the final report of the IPPR Media and Communication project. These include:

> To suppress publication, ie prior restraint, it must be shown that the utterance presents a clear and present danger that cannot retrospectively be remedied.
>
> To punish publication of material it must be shown that a harm has been committed which merits action.
>
> To restrict minors' access to material actual harm need not be shown but the protection of minors should not deny adults access to material to which they otherwise have lawful access.
>
> To restrict material on behalf of adults, it must be shown that reasonable people are likely to be offended by the material.

Unlike the Williams Committee (and Professor Williams succinctly outlined his Committee's thinking on this issue in his paper), we believe that there are reasons to retain a public interest defence for publication of material that would otherwise be unlawful. Williams reasonably proposed that pornographic material which showed criminal acts should be suppressed. But, however desirable suppression of representations of sadism, non-consensual sex or child sex might seem there are circumstances in which such representations might serve legitimate ends. "Violence, cruelty or horror" was abundantly present in the Holocaust yet images documenting the crimes attending the "Final Solution" would, using the Williams Committee criteria, be suppressed. Here the importance of retaining a public interest defence seems palpable. Moreover, the difficulties of establishing from the evidence of a representation what was a record of an actual criminal act and what was an imitation of criminal action should not be underestimated. Films such as "The Accused" depict simulated rape but cannot be thought to incite, promote or legitimise sexual violence. Sensitive judgements will continue to be required of regulators.

Because content regulation is judgemental the selection, accountability and representativeness of the "gatekeepers" who decide on our behalf what is to be restricted and suppressed is of the essence. Neither the composition of the current gatekeepers of media content nor the institutional configuration through which they exercise their regulatory authority provide grounds for confidence. Accordingly, regulatory arrangements need changing. Proposals have been canvassed at an IPPR seminar whose proceedings will be published early in 1996 and will inform recommendations to be made in the final report of the IPPR media and communications project.

Endnotes

1 Home Office, Report of the Committee on Obscenity and Film Censorship London (1979) HMSO November 1979 Cmnd 7772

2 Itzin C (1992) *Pornography: Women, Violence and Civil Liberties*, Oxford University Press

3 "The Gatekeepers. Who Regulates Media Content?", IPPR *mimeo* (1995) Undertaken for the IPPR Media and Communication Project by Adam Jacobs, London

DELIBERATE LEWDNESS AND THE CREATIVE IMAGINATION:

should we censor pornography?

Erica Jong

> The form of government most suitable to the artist is no government at all.
>
> Oscar Wilde

We live in a time when the freedom to publish sexually-oriented material is coming under attack, when large publishing conglomerates increasingly control all means of communication, and when the forces of cultural reaction are becoming extremely well-organized. The brief cultural glasnost of the sixties is beginning to seem quaint. At such a juncture it is particularly important to re-examine what constitutes forbidden material in literature and to cut through the political grandstanding about its supposed evils in order to understand what purpose it actually serves in society. If nothing else, we should try to grasp what motivates the creators and consumers of it.

Pornographic material has been present in the art and literature of every society in every historical period. What has changed from epoch to epoch–or even from one decade to another–is the ability of such material to flourish publicly and to be distributed legally. In elitist societies there are, paradoxically, fewer calls for censorship than in democratic ones, since elitist societies function as *de facto* censors, keeping certain materials out the purview of Hoi Polloi. As democracy increases, so does the demand for legal control over the erotic, the pornographic, the scatological. Our own century is a perfect example of the oscillations of taste regarding such material. We have gone from the banning and burning of D. H. Lawrence, James Joyce, Radclyffe Hall, Henry Miller and other avant garde artists early in the century, to a passionate struggle to free literature from censorship in mid-century, to a new wave of reaction at century's end.

After nearly a hundred years of agitating for freedom to publish, we find that the enemies of freedom have multiplied, rather than diminished.

They are Christians, Muslims, oppressive totalitarian regimes, even well-meaning social libertarians who happen to be feminists, teachers, school boards, librarians. This should not surprise us since, as Margaret Mead pointed out 40 years ago, the demand for state censorship is usually "a response to the presence within the society of heterogeneous groups of people with differing standards and aspirations."[1] As our culture becomes more diverse, we can expect more calls for censorship rather than fewer. So it is essential for us to understand what role pornography plays in our lives and what value it has.

Our job is made tougher and more confusing by the fact that the spate of freedoms we briefly enjoyed in the late sixties, the seventies and the early eighties led to the proliferation of sexual materials so ugly, exploitative and misogynistic that it is difficult to defend them. The door was opened to *Lolita*, *Lady Chatterley's Lover*, *Tropic of Cancer*, *Couples*, *Portnoy's Complaint*, *Fear of Flying*, but it was also opened to *Debbie does Dallas*, *Deep Throat*, and an array of printed and filmed pornography so offensive to women that it has understandably provoked the ire of feminists. Pornography also became hugely profitable once legal restraints were lifted and this in turn gave rise to another wave of reaction.

We stand at a crossroads now when many former libertarians and liberals suddenly want to ban sexual materials. The old dream of the avant garde that freeing sexual oppression would free human beings from their inhibitions and limitations has withered. We think we are sadder and wiser about what sexual freedom leads to, but in truth we never really tried sexual freedom. We only ballyhooed its simulacrum. I want to bypass a reappraisal of the so-called sexual revolution for the moment and look instead at the impulse to create pornography and the role it plays in works of art. We owe it to ourselves to understand the impulses toward pornography, eroticism, scatology, before resuming our contentious public debate about their uses and whether or not they should be restricted. I use the terms eroticism and pornography interchangeably because I have come to the conclusion that only snobbery divides them. At one time I thought of pornography as purely an aid to masturbation and eroticism as something more high-toned and spiritual, like Molly Bloom's soliloquy in *Ulysses*. Now I doubt that division. Every visual artist - from the anonymous sculptor of the bare-breasted Minoan snake goddess to Pompeii's brothel muralists to William Turner and Pablo

Picasso – has been drawn to the erotic and the pornographic. So have literary artists throughout human history. Sometimes the urge has been to stimulate the genitals; sometimes the urge has been to stimulate the mind. Since the mind and the genitals are part of one organism, why distinguish between masturbatory dreams and aesthetic ones? Surely there is also an aesthetics of masturbation which our society is too sex-negative to explore. At any rate, it is time to go back to the origin of the pornographic impulse and explore the reasons why it is so tenacious.

Mark Twain's *1601* is a perfect place to start. Although Mark Twain lived in the Victorian age and knew he could never publish his pornographic fancies officially, they nevertheless preoccupied his energies and he was so proud of them that he sought to disseminate them among his friends. In Mark Twain's case, pornography was an essential part of his oeuvre because it primed the pump for other sorts of freedom of expression. It allowed him to fly free in creating a new sort of American vernacular, first-person narratives that drew on American speech patterns and revealed the soul of America as never before. Experiments with pornography, scatology, eroticism allowed him to delve into the communal unconscious and create some of the most profound myths on which American culture is based.

Twain's 1601. Conversation As It Was By The Social Fireside, In The Time Of The Tudors fascinates me because it demonstrates Mark Twain's passion for linguistic experiment and how allied it is with his compulsion toward "deliberate lewdness". The phrase "deliberate lewdness" is Vladimir Nabokov's. In a witty Afterword to his groundbreaking 1955 novel *Lolita*, he links the urge to create pornography with "the verve of a fine poet in a wanton mood"[2] and regrets that "in modern times the term 'pornography' connotes mediocrity, commercialism, and certain strict rules of narration." In contemporary porn, Nabokov says, "action has to be limited to the copulation of clichés." Poetry is always out of the question. "Style, structure, imagery should never distract the reader from his tepid lust." Motivated by such lacklustre lust, the connoisseur of pornography is impatient with all attempts at verbal dexterity and linguistic wit. One is reminded that Henry Miller failed miserably as a paid pornographer because he could not leave the poetry out as his anonymous patron wished. Anaïs Nin fared better with *Delta of Venus* and *Little Birds*. For Henry Miller pornography mattered precisely because it aroused him to poetry!

Henry Miller's attitude toward the pornographic is an ancient one. Poetry and pornography went hand in hand in Roman, Renaissance and eighteenth-century literature. The pornographic flights of Catullus, Ovid, Petronius and Juvenal never sacrificed style. Boccaccio, Villon, Rabelais, Cervantes, Shakespeare, John Donne and Andrew Marvell, all delighted in making porn poetic. Jonathan Swift, Alexander Pope and Lawrence Sterne were equally drunk with lewdness and with language.No creator should have to bother about "the exact demarcation between the sensuous and the sensual," says Nabokov. Let the censors worry about such hypocritical distinctions. The literary artist has another agenda: to free the imagination and let the wildness of the mind go free. Nabokov is, of course, defending his own offspring *Lolita*, that light of his loins and pen which caused such consternation that it could not at first be published anywhere but in Paris by Maurice Girodias' Olympia Press. The pornographic verve of ancient literature was his inspiration: in this he would have recognised Mark Twain as a brother.

In choosing to write from the point of view of "the Pepys of that day, the same being cup-bearer to Queen Elizabeth" in *1601*, Mark Twain was transporting himself to a world that existed before the invention of sexual hypocrisy. The Elizabethans were openly bawdy. They found bodily functions funny and sex arousing to the muse. Restoration wits and Augustan satirists had the same openness to bodily functions and the same respect for Eros. Only in the nineteenth century did prudery (and the threat of legal censure) begin to paralyse the author's hand. Shakespeare, Rochester and Pope were far more fettered politically than we are, but the fact was that they were not required to put condoms on their pens when the matter of sex arose. They were pleased to remind their readers of the essential messiness of the body. They followed a classical tradition that often expressed moral indignation through scatology. "Oh Celia, Celia, Celia shits,"[3] writes Swift, as if she were the first woman in history to do so. In his so-called "unprintable poems", Swift is debunking the conventions of courtly love (as well as expressing his own deep misogyny) but he is doing so in a spirit that Catullus and Juvenal would have recognised. The satirist lashes the world to bring the world to its senses. It does the dance of the satyrs around our follies.

Twain's scatology serves this purpose as well, but it is also a warm-up for his creative process. Stuck in the prudish nineteenth century, Mark Twain craved the freedom of the ancients. In championing "deliberate lewdness" in 1601, he bestowed the gift of freedom on himself. Even more interesting is the fact that Mark Twain was writing *1601* during the very same summer (1876) that he was "tearing along on a new book" – the first 16 chapters of a novel he then referred to as "Huck Finn's Autobiography". This conjunction is hardly coincidental. *1601* and *Huckleberry Finn* have a great deal in common besides linguistic experimentation. According to Justin Kaplan "both were implicit rejections of the taboos and codes of polite society and both were experiments in using the vernacular as a literary medium."[4]

What exactly is the connection between *Huck Finn* and *1601*? As a professional writer whose process of composition often resembles Twain's (intermittent work on ambitious novels, writing blocks during which I put one work aside and devote myself to other projects, and periods of lecturing and travel), I think I understand Twain's creative strategy. He was sneaking up on the muse so that she would not be forewarned and escape. Every author knows that a book only begins to live when the voice of its narrator comes alive. You may have plot ideas, characters may haunt you in the night, but the book does not fly until the sound of its voice is heard in the author's ear. And the sound of one book's voice is as individual as the sound of a child's voice. It may be related to that of other offspring, but it always has its own particular timbre, its own particular quirks.

In order to find the true voice of the book, the author must be free to play without fear of reprisals. All writing blocks come from excessive self-judgment, the internalised voice of the critical parent telling the author's imagination that it is a dirty little boy or girl. "Hah!" says the author, "I will flaunt the voice of parental propriety and break free!" This is why pornographic spirit is always related to unhampered creativity. Artists are fascinated with filth because we know that in filth, everything human is born. Human beings emerge between piss and shit and so do novels and poems. Only by letting go of the inhibition that makes us bow to social propriety can we delve into the depths of the unconscious. We assert our freedom with pornographic play. If we are lucky, we keep that freedom long enough to create a masterpiece like *Huckleberry Finn.*

But the two compulsions are more than just related; they are causally intertwined. When *Huckleberry Finn* was published in 1885, Louisa May Alcott put her finger on exactly what mattered about the novel even as she condemned it: "If Mr. Clemens cannot think of something better to tell our pure-minded lads and lasses, he had best stop writing for them."[5] What Alcott didn't know was that "our pure-minded lads and lasses" aren't. But Mark Twain knew. It is not at all surprising that during that summer of high scatological spirits Twain should also give birth to the irreverent voice of Huck. If *Little Women* fails to go as deep as Twain's masterpiece, it is precisely because of Alcott's concern with puremindedness. Niceness is ever the enemy of art. If you worry about what the neighbours, critics, parents and supposedly pureminded censors think, you will never create a work that defies the restrictions of the conscious mind and delves into the world of dreams.

1601 is deliberately lewd. It delights in stinking up the air of propriety. It delights in describing great thundergusts of farts which make great stenches and pricks which are stiff until cunts "take ye stiffness out of them."[6] In the midst of all this ribaldry, the assembled company speaks of many things – poetry, theatre, art, politics. Twain knew that the muse flies on the wings of flatus, and he was having such a good time writing this Elizabethan pastiche that the humour shines through a 120 years later. I dare you to read *1601* without giggling and guffawing.

In the last few years a great deal of pious politically correct garbage has been written about pornography. Pornography, the high-minded self-anointed feminist Catherine Mackinnon tells us, is tantamount to an assault on women and causes rape.[7] Pornography, asserts Mackinnon's comrade-in-arms Andrea Dworkin, is a form of rape.[8] Clare Short asserts that pictures of naked women in tabloids are to blame for women's unhappiness in love and inequity in finances. A chorus of younger feminists at last has come along to counter these unexamined contentions. Pornography, says Susie Bright,[9] is necessary to liberation. Pornography, says Sallie Tisdale,[10] is desired by women as well as men. Pornography, says Nadine Strossen,[11] is guaranteed by the Bill of Rights.

But what about the Bill of Rights for artists? Could Robert Mapplethorpe's photographs of lilies have existed without his photographs of pricks? Could Henry Miller have grasped human transcendence in *The Colossus of Maroussi* without having wallowed in the sewers of Paris in *Tropic of Cancer*?

I say no. Without farts, there are no flowers. Without pricks, there are no poems.

This is not the first time in history we have seen an essentially libertarian movement like feminism devolve into a debate about puremindedness. The suffragists of the last century also turned into prudish prohibitionists who spent their force proscribing drink and policing puremindedness. One might argue that a concern with puremindedness is not only fatal to art but also to political movements. Why does this urge toward repression crop up in supposedly libertarian movements? And why does this puritanical urge to censor the artist keep recurring? The artist needs to be free to play in the id in order to bring back insights for the ego. But the id is scary. It yawns like a bottomless vagina dentata. It threatens to bite off heads, hands, cocks, and to swallow us up in our own darkest impulses. Society fears the id even as it yearns for the release to be found there.[12] We retreat from dream and fantasy even as we long to submerge in them. Make no mistake about it: the primal ooze of creation is terrifying. It reminds us of how little control we have over our lives, over our deaths. It reminds us of our origins and inspires us to contemplate our inevitable annihilation.

Pornographic art is perceived as dangerous to political movements because, like the unconscious, it is not programmable. It is dangerous play whose outcome never can be predicted. Since dream is the speech of the unconscious, the artist who would create works of value must be fluent in speaking the language of dream. The pornographic has a direct connection to the unconscious. I suspect this was why Twain was having such fun with *1601* the very summer Huck Finn's adventures were burgeoning in his brain. The filth of 1601 fertilised the garden of Huck's adventures. Like any literary artist who is in touch with his id, Twain instinctively knew that sex and creativity were interrelated. He could not fill *Huckleberry Finn* with farts, pricks and cunts, but he could play in *1601* and prepare his imagination for the antisocial adventures he would give his anti-hero in the other book.

In his classic essay, *Obscenity and The Law of Reflection*,[13] Henry Miller suggests that "when obscenity crops out in art, in literature more particularly, it usually functions as a technical device... Its purpose is to awaken, to usher in a sense of reality. In a sense, its use by the artist may be compared to the use of the miraculous by the Masters..." Here Miller means the spiritual masters. He believed that Christ and the zen masters only resorted to miracles when such were absolutely necessary to awaken their disciples. The artist uses obscenity the same way. "The real nature of the obscene lies in its lust to convert," Miller says. Obscenity is used in literature as a sort of wake-up call to the unconscious. Obscenity transports us to "another dimension of reality".

So *1601* served an important creative function for its author. It awakened his freedom to experiment, play, and dream outrageous dreams. Havelock Ellis once said that "adults need obscene literature, as much as children need fairy tales, as a relief from the obsessive force of convention." The urge toward obscenity is nothing more or less than the urge toward freedom. Those who condemn it are clearly afraid of the debauchery that freedom might unleash in themselves. They inevitably condemn what they are most attracted to. The censor is the one who slavers in private over books, films and visual artifacts which he or she then proscribes for the rest of society. Throughout history, the urge to censor has always been strongest in those most attracted to the freedom of the obscene. In quashing freedom in others, the censor hopes to quash it within. "Liberation," says Henry Miller, "implies the sloughing off of chains, the bursting of the cocoon. What is obscene are the preliminary or anticipatory movements of birth, the preconscious writhing in the face of a life to be."

Miller goes on to say that the obscene "is an attempt to spy on the secret processes of the universe." The guilt of the creator when he or she knows that something extraordinary is being born, comes from the knowledge of tampering with God-like powers, a Promethean guilt for impersonating the immortals. "The obscene has all the qualities of the hidden interval," Miller says:

> It is vast as the Unconscious itself and as amorphous and fluid as the very stuff of the Unconscious. It is what comes to the surface as strange, intoxicating and forbidden, and which therefore arrests and paralyses, when in the form of

> Narcissus we bend over our own image in the mirror of our own iniquity. Acknowledged by all, it is nevertheless despised and rejected, wherefore it is constantly emerging in Protean guise at the most unexpected moments. When it is recognised and accepted... it inspires no more dread than... the flowering lotus which sends its roots down into the mud of the stream of which it is borne.

Sexuality and creativity were not always divorced as they are today and as they were in Mark Twain's day. All so-called "primitive" and "pagan" art exhibits the marriage of sexuality and creativity – whether in the form of giant phalluses, multitudinous breasts or pregnant bellies. But the divorce between body and mind that characterises the Christian era has led the artist to curious strategies of creation and constant guilt for the possession of the creative gift. We see this guilt as clearly in Mark Twain as in any artist who ever lived. His creative strategies of intermittent composition, his fear of working on a book once it became clear that the process of composition would inevitably lift the veil and take him into the sacred and forbidden precincts, betrays his hypersensitivity to something we might call post-Christian-creator-guilt – if it weren't such a daunting mouthful.

In so-called "primitive" societies, the artist and the shaman are one. There is no discontinuity between artistic creation and the sacred. The shaman-artist creates in order to worship and worships in order to create. Not so the artist in our culture. Always wracked by guilt for the power of creativity itself, beset by censors within and without, our artists are shackled by a sense of transgression so deep it often destroys them. No wonder we use obscenity to break open the door, to lift the veil. No wonder we insist on our right to do so as if our lives depended on it. They do.

So the artist needs pornography as a way into the unconscious, and history proves that if this license is not granted, it will be stolen.

Mark Twain had *1601* privately printed. Picasso kept pornographic notebooks that were only exhibited after his death. But what about access to these works? Should access be restricted? And if so, how shall we decide to whom it shall be restricted and how shall we decide who makes the decision? As I said earlier, this is a problem that only arises in heterogeneous societies. In homogeneous societies, tradition and taboo govern what shall be seen and what unseen and the whole tribe agrees about it. There is no problem. But our society is multi-ethnic, multi-racial, multi-sexual. What is offensive to a Muslim may not be offensive to a unitarian. What is offensive to an Orthodox Jew may not be offensive to an assimilated Jew. What is offensive to a feminist may seem like free speech to a lusty male adolescent. We do not even agree on the definition of obscenity. Who shall make rules for the whole of society when society is so diverse and none of us agrees on the definition of obscenity?

This is the problem we confront today. Add to it the relentlessly commercial thrust of our communications media and the fact that they are concentrated in fewer and fewer hands, and you see the danger we are in. Commercial television networks in America have "solved" the problem by editing out anything that may be offensive to any group who may petition their sponsors. Ban what is quirky, eccentric, imaginative, sexual, satirical or strange and the result will be the predigested baby formula American television offers. The whole country is in danger of becoming a Disney theme-park whose main aim is to sell hamburgers, hotdogs and copyrighted trinkets in the shapes of cartoon characters. So-called "interactive media" – whose main interaction is that of credit card and telephone order taker – seems to be going the same way. Something called the Communications Decency Act is now pending before the Congress of the United States. It will ban sex in cyberspace, but apparently not selling. Selling is, of course, not considered obscene in America.

Margaret Mead says that all societies have two problems in relation to sex:

> how to keep sex activity out of forbidden channels that will endanger the bodies and souls of others or the co-operative processes of social life, and how to keep it flowing reliably in those channels where it is a necessity if children are to be conceived and reared in homes where father and mother are tied together by the requisite amount of sexual interest.

We must keep people together to rear families and we must raise children who can "focus their capacities for sexual feelings on particular persons." These two social tasks seem simple to effect, but they are not. Random sexual activity must be controlled, contained, ritualised – but not to the detriment of desire itself. Desire is necessary – not only for art but for binding parents together. Sex can be a destructive force or a cohesive one – depending on how it is used. Many so-called "primitive" societies have allowed group sexual activities under particular circumstances – to propitiate the crops or to celebrate a wedding or feast. "An orgy for all which serves group goals ceases to be an orgy, and so is dignified," says Margaret Mead.

One of the reasons we are so negative toward pornography is because we do not see pornography as serving group goals. In this, we may be mistaken. The former US Surgeon General, Jocelyn Elders, was recently forced to step down after publicly averring that masturbation might be a good thing for adolescents – a far better thing than early sexual activity and parenthood. Such is the still prevalent sexual hypocrisy of my country that this eminently sensible statement caused an outcry. And President Clinton, he-who-did-not-inhale, forced her to resign. I cheered her. Any idiot can see that masturbation is less harmful than parenthood at 12, 13, 14, 15... But one may not say so publicly in America. We are supposed to pretend that sexual desire does not exist. Sexual desire does exist and every society in history has expressed it in art, literature, jokes, dances, music, sacred rituals. Now we are faced with the possibility that the heterogeneity of our society may lead to our banning those universal expressions of human feeling.

I believe that censorship is always an evil to be deplored in a free society. A far better method of keeping inappropriate materials out of the purview of those we deem too young or too emotionally vulnerable for them is a system of rating or labelling visual or literary materials so that minors and those who seek to protect them can be forewarned. To restrict access to materials by age is not the same as to proscribe them. Parents who believe it is their responsibility to protect their children from the corruptions of television, movies, books and the Internet have but to pull the plug on the machine (or lock up the books and magazines) when danger beckons. It is unfair for such parents to demand that the state control what they themselves cannot control. So too with puritanical sects. If they cannot dissuade their youths from wallowing in what is morally corrupting, what kind of moral leadership are they providing? Surely they cannot demand that the state provide for them the moral authority their priests cannot provide?

In place of censorship I would limit access, increase parental responsibility, and urge those who do not like our mass media to create their own competing media. If we ban whatever offends any group in our diverse society, we will soon have no art, no culture, no humour, no satire. Satire is by its nature offensive. So is much art and political discourse. The value of these expressions far outweighs their risk. Oscar Wilde – who appears to have said everything – said of censorship:

> In France... they limit the journalist and allow the artist almost perfect freedom. Here we allow absolute freedom to the journalist and limit the artist.

In 1995, the centenary of Wilde's sentencing for "gross indecency", we ought to be wiser about restricting sexual expression than our predecessors were. In the name of protecting children, we cannot starve adults. In the name of social harmony, we cannot ban ecstasy. We can limit access based on age. I believe that is the most we should do. The enforcement may be spotty – but so too is the enforcement on banning nicotine for children. As long as we allow tobacco companies to addict our children to a cancer-causing substance, it is sheer hypocrisy to demand censorship of sexual materials on the grounds that they pervert and corrupt. No one has proven this perversion and corruption. On the contrary, the carcinogens in cigarettes has been proven. The well-meaning feminists who assert without evidence that pornography is rape, the evangelical Christians whose influence over their own children is so weak they want the state to bolster them, the Muslims who read everything literally and thus proclaim *fatwas* against creative writers, cannot be our masters. Our concern must be with keeping intellectual and artistic excellence alive even in a pluralistic democracy. It is a tough challenge and it tends to bring out the zealotry in the most academic ideologues. "Every idea is an incitement," said Oliver Wendell Holmes. Surely that does not mean we should banish ideas.

English law on the subject of pornography attempts to ban certain materials on the basis of their tendency "to deprave and corrupt". The so-called Hicklin rule on which nearly all British and American pornography decisions were based for over a century (and which has recently been revived by Catherine Mackinnon under another name) made the test for obscenity its tendency to "deprave and corrupt those whose minds are open to such immoral influences." The Obscene Publications Act of 1959 and 1964 modified Hicklin but still relied on the test of depraving and corrupting to define pornography and to distinguish it from those productions of human ingenuity which advance medical science or art or literature. We must admit that this is an inexact test, very prone to influence by political trends. The current United States law on pornography is equally bad. It asserts "community standards" as a test and begs the question of federal standards entirely.

So we are no closer to a good definition of obscenity than we ever were, and as our society grows more diverse, we are in for more chaos and confusion. If you factor in the problem that so-called defenders of public morality are not always entirely sincere and are often motivated by low political ambitions, you see how thorny the dilemma is. In his recent memoir, *Murderers and Other Friends*, John Mortimer has a witty passage about this very subject:

> As defenders, we naturally found ourselves on the side of books and films which the prosecution was trying to ban. That didn't mean that we found these works particularly attractive; it's not necessary, when defending an alleged murderer, to believe that the best way to end an unhappy marriage is with a kitchen knife in the stomach. Prosecutors who seek to keep the purity of our national life unsullied can be similarly detached. Geoff and I did a long case about some questioned publication or other against a particularly jovial prosecutor who would push his way past my middle-aged knees every morning and chirrup, 'Give us a kiss, darling,' as I sat gloomily preparing my work for the day. I used to write in a number of notebooks which had dark circles printed on their covers. In his final speech to the jury this prosecutor was saying, 'And if this sort of publication is allowed, youth will be corrupted, authority will be undermined, family life will be in peril and civilisation, as we know it, will grind to a halt.' Then, glancing down at my notebook, he muttered, 'Arseholes all over your notebook, darling!', and went on with his peroration. The truth is that the defenders of public morality are not always all that they seem to be.

Indeed not. We have to admit that history of censorship from Anthony Comstock to the present has not been a distinguished one. Moreover, people being people, and motivated by power first, lust second, there is an imperishable human tendency to use censorship for political ends: to crush one's opponents, to keep dissenters silent, to prevent changes in the status quo, to keep women properly in their place. Whenever and wherever legal grounds for censorship exist, it is never long before they are used to crush the underdog, the non-conformist, the woman, the witch. Because censorship is such an obvious club put in the hands of the state, I am mystified by feminists who seek to renew its force. Perhaps they believe they are (or are soon to be) the state – in which case they are seriously deluded. A concern with "public morality" is – if not the last refuge of a scoundrel – the first foray of the fascist. First they burn books, as Heinrich Heine said, then they burn people. For "books" – read films, Internet, television, whatever.

And who profits from censorship? I maintain that those who own and control the fewer and fewer media conglomerates do. Through censorship laws, their hegemony over the airwaves, over the Internet is protected. The Christian Coalition will at first seek to control the Internet with anti-obscenity laws, but you can be sure that their definition of obscenity will not include rallying militia movements via optical fibre, nor proselytising against gun-control laws, environmental regulation, freedom of contraceptive choice and abortion. One's enemy's agenda is always obscene. One's own is always moral. For this reason alone, I am against censorship. I prefer the chaos of uncontrollable communication of all sorts to selective banning of certain materials. I do not think human beings can be trusted to be above politics and to promote the common good. One group's common good is another group's evil.

We are better off punishing rapists, making our streets safe for women and children, than banning pornography. We are better off spending time raising our children and teaching them values than attempting to police television, magazines, the Internet. I suspect that calls for censorship are always the lazy person's way of influencing the minds of the young. The truth is we teach our children by our own example and not by what we let them watch on television or plug into on the net. If we are hypocrites, they will be hypocrites too. If we are honest about our beliefs, they will be drawn to honesty as well. Mass communications do not raise our children; we do. In attempting to control the airwaves, we are (unwittingly perhaps) mimicking Rupert Murdoch's, Ted Turner's, and Silvio Berlusconi's agenda. We are making our media safe for selling, delivering the next generation of customers, and abdicating our own personal responsibility. Better to turn the television off than to turn off our own discrimination, parenting, and judgment.

The calls for censorship we have lately heard are an attempt to blame mass communications for all the seemingly unsoluble problems of a violent and over-populated world where wealth has increasingly become the only measure of worth. The truth is that mass communications are but a mirror of our values. They only show us who we are and what we have become. If we dislike what we see there, we should cure the diseased body politic, not merely attempt to retouch its image. That is a way of doing nothing while reassuring ourselves of our zeal for reform.

Endnotes

1 Mead M (1953) "A Sex and Censorship in Contemporary Society", *New World Writing*, The New American Library of World Literature Inc., New York

2 Nabokov V (1955) "On a Book entitled Lolita", *Lolita*, G. P. Putnam's Sons, New York, NY

3 Swift J (1760) "The Lady's Dressing Room" [1730] in *Swift's Works* Vol VII. Hitch, Hawes *et al*, London

4 Kaplan J (1966) *Mr. Clemens and Mark Twain*, Simon and Schuster, New York

5 Alcott L M quoted by Justin Kaplan (*ibid*) p268

6 Twain M (1992) *1601. Conversation, as it Was by the Social Fireside, in the Time of the Tudors*, Literary Classics of the United States Inc., New York

7 Mackinnon C (1993) *Only Words*, Harvard University Press, Cambridge

8 Dworkin A (1993) *Letters From A War Zone*, Lawrence Hill Books, Brooklyn

9 Susie Bright expounds her views on pornography in many of her books. Some representative titles are: *Sexual Reality: A Virtual Sex World Reader* (1992) Cleis Press, San Francisco, California. *Herotica 3* (1994) Plume Books, New York. *Sexwise* (1995) Cleis Press, Pittsburgh, Pennsylvania

10 Tisdale S (1994) *Talk Dirty To Me*, Doubleday, New York

11 Strossen N (1995) *Defending Pornography. Free speech, sex and the fight for women's rights* Scribners

12 Mead M, *ibid*

13 Miller H (1964) "Obscenity and the Law of Reflection" in *Henry Miller on Writing*, New Directions Publishing Corporation, New York

SUPPRESSION AND RESTRICTION OF PORNOGRAPHY:
long spoons and the supper of the righteous

Bernard Williams

I shall start from the recommendations of the Committee on Obscenity and Film Censorship of which I was Chairman, and which reported in 1979. It is a long time ago now, but I do not think that our recommendations are irrelevant.

The word "obscenity" got into the name of this committee because it is a technical term in the English law, being defined there in terms of a tendency to deprave and corrupt. I do not want to say anything about that definition on this occasion, though it is extensively discussed in the report. I shall stick mostly to the term "pornography". I do not regard the term "pornography" as itself a value term. In this I coincide, I think, with what Erica Jong says. I do not agree with her that there is no distinction between pornography and the erotic: I think that clearly there are erotic works of art that are not pornographic and there are pornographic objects that are not erotic. But I do agree with her in the substance of her point, namely that the distinction between the erotic and the pornographic is not simply a value distinction: the erotic is not simply, as it were, posh pornography.

I stand by the main recommendations of our report, and they still seem to me sensible. The law in Britain has not in fact been changed as a result of our report, except in minor respects, though practice has undoubtedly come nearer to what we recommended. The main recommendations were these. Firstly, one could not commit an offence under this title at all with a work that consisted entirely of the printed word; the printed word would be neither banned nor restricted for reasons concerned with pornography. Secondly, a small class of works could actually be suppressed. Suppression, I think, is what Erica Jong and others mean by the term "censorship", but the term is ambiguous. It can mean total suppression or attempted suppression of certain kinds of publications, or it can mean any attempt to control them. I therefore shall not use the word "censorship", but rather the two terms that we used in the report, "suppression" and "restriction".

Suppression, first of all, means that the law tries to bring it about that a work shall not be circulated at all; its publication is made, ex-post, illegal. We recommended suppression only for material where there was a presumption that a crime was committed in the course of making it; that is to say, acts that were involved when the pornography was manufactured were themselves criminal acts. This meant, roughly, acts of genuine sadism and child pornography. (There are some problems with this definition, but they are fairly detailed questions which I do not think need detain us on this occasion.) The basic point is that one can suppress a work only in cases where there is a crime which would be a crime anyway, whether or not it gave rise to a publication. What will have happened in such a case is that a crime, of a sexual nature, has been filmed or photographed, for the purposes of producing pornography.

The more wide-ranging part of the report concerned the proposals with regard to restriction. There are two questions here. First, what does "restriction" mean? Roughly speaking, material is restricted if it can be sold only in certain kinds of premises, it is not displayed in an open manner to members of the public who do not want to see it, and access to it is denied to children. It means, in effect, that the material is confined to sex shops. There is then the difficult question of the criterion for being something that should be restricted. Our idea was that restriction should be applied to material which was "offensive". As we discovered in the course of our very long discussions on this subject, the matter of defining such offensiveness in a manner that could actually work in a court of law is harder than one might think. We came up with the proposal that matter should be restricted – and I quote – "which, not consisting of the written word, is such that its unrestricted availability is offensive to reasonable people by reason of the manner in which it portrays, deals with or relates to violence, cruelty or horror, or sexual, faecal or urinary functions or genital organs". I do not now think that this is exactly right, but I think that it is not bad.

The fundamental idea behind the proposal of restriction – that is to say, of the requirement that these materials be sold and displayed only under certain controlled conditions to volunteer adults – is that the offensiveness of publicly-displayed pornography is an extension of the offensiveness of publicly-displayed sexual activity. That is, the objection to it is fundamentally to a violation of the boundary between public and private.

Thus, pornography is found offensive if publicly displayed even if the material that is displayed in it, the acts that have been photographed, are of a perfectly ordinary and respectable kind – for instance, if they consist of perfectly straight sex between a married couple. Now, presumably nobody thinks that this activity itself should be made illegal. It may be objectionable, however, if it is going on in public, and, to come to the case of pornography, there will be an objection if photographs of it are forced on the public attention. A further step is taken when the material of the pornography is the material of fantasy, which may be entertained in private but becomes a different thing when it is displayed in public.

Such displays are found offensive by many people. Our view was that for various psychological reasons this offensiveness may go quite deep and that it should not be despised. It is a perfectly reasonable reaction, and there is no reason why such activities or photographs of such activities should be forced upon people's attention. It is a reasonable demand that such material should be restricted, though not that it should be banned or suppressed. Offensiveness should be taken seriously, but taking it seriously does not mean that the material should be suppressed, as opposed to being restricted to a volunteer adult public.

The formulation we proposed spells out, in its rather cumbrous way, the reason for the restriction, namely that the material is pornographic. That is why the list of conditions mentioning sexual organs and so on gets into it. There is a special reason for this, namely that the notion of offensiveness involved has got to be pinned down to the kind of offensiveness that is involved in being confronted with overt sexual materials. If one simply said that material can be restricted which is found offensive by many persons, then the way is open to restricting material which is offensive in virtue of the opinions it expresses. We took the view that even restriction, that is to say, confining the material to a volunteer public, would be inappropriate for material that was offensive simply in terms of the opinions it expressed, because of course a lot of opinions are offensive to a lot of people, and a restriction to a volunteer public would be an undue restriction on freedom of speech.

However, I now think that the formula we adopted did not quite capture what we wanted. We said that the material in question was such that "its unrestricted availability is offensive..." The reason for putting it in this way was two-fold. On the one hand, we wanted to allow for the fact that material which reasonable people would find offensive when publicly displayed might not be offensive to them if they viewed it in private. What we meant by our formula was material that is offensive to reasonable people, when it is unrestrictedly available. At the same time, however, we wanted to allow for the possibility that some material, even if it displayed the listed sexual features, should be allowed for reasons of the public interest – for news or medical purposes, for instance, and we hoped to allow for this also under the one formula "such that its unrestricted availability is offensive..." But that is a muddle, since the formula could only serve this second purpose if the offensiveness in question is taken to operate at the level of opinions, and that is not the level at which we wanted it to be understood if it was to fulfil its primary function. This problem, if it is a problem, should be dealt with by other means.

An important feature of the definition is the use of the phrase "reasonable people". That phrase is used elsewhere in the law, and that is why we used it. The law often refers to things that would be foreseen by reasonable people, expected by reasonable people and so on, and what this signals is the avoidance of extremes, either of the reckless or the neurotically cautious. So in this case, in thinking whether something is offensive if publicly displayed, you do not take the point of view either of the most puritanical and squeamish on the one hand, nor of the depraved libertine peruser of pornographer on the other, but something in the middle. This works in one sense in that it allows for some relativity to different outlooks, and so to different communities in different locations: what will be offensive if displayed in the middle of a country village might not be so on 8th Avenue or in the Charing Cross Road.

However, the formula will not deal with different outlooks in the same location: if there are persons who are very easily offended and other persons of a tougher temperament who are living in the same place, then the determination of what is reasonable will be a problem. The answer to this, I am afraid, is that it is a problem, and there is simply no way in which anybody can get round it by legislation. What you cannot do is legislate for dictatorship by the most puritanical group. If there are, for example, four persons of extreme sensitivity who belong to a sect which cannot bear any picture of a woman appearing in underwear in any form of magazine, one cannot rule that all such magazines should be stripped from the shops of the places where those persons live or are likely to go. That is clearly a non-starter. If the community is so heterogeneous that there never can be an agreement on this, then indeed there is a problem, but it cannot be solved by the law.

The last point I should like to make about our recommendations is one for which I think that the argument is particularly clear. The present English law allows a so-called "public good defence" on grounds such as literary and artistic merit against conviction on obscenity. It is an interesting fact about this provision that it does not make clear, nor does the jury have to decide, whether a successful public good defence on these grounds means that the work is not obscene, or merely says that, although it is obscene, it should not be convicted. Those who introduced the Obscene Publications Act, and with good intentions brought in this defence, apparently thought it better, no doubt wisely, that the Act should not commit itself on this point. Our Committee came to the conclusion, which none of us expected when we started but we all agreed with when we finished, that the public good defence, though in practice it did valuable work in its time, simply does not make sense. Fundamentally, the idea of the public good defence is that experts from the world of culture should appear before a court of law and under hostile examination by a barrister persuade a jury that a book which has just been published has literary merit. This in itself is a remarkable achievement for a set of professors or critics to bring off. But, in any case, the provision involves a basic fault of principle, that it can only defend works that are artistically successful. But what has to be defended is not success but experiment, and so it must be possible to defend works that are unsuccessful. The publisher cannot be in the position of saying "it will be all right if it's a masterpiece, otherwise we can't publish it". The artistic merit clause has simply got to be dropped, and we must accept the consequences of this, that if we do not want to prosecute the valuable, we had better be cautious about what we prosecute.

Let me say something briefly about how far any legislation on this general line can be applied in the technological conditions that have developed since we reported. This particularly concerns, it seems to me, satellite and Internet, and, in particular, Internet. I regard the problems about this as rather more severe than Erica Jong does. The idea of restriction rules is both to stop offence to adults who do not want to see such material and to keep it away from children. The material is to be in a place where adults who do not wish to see it do not come across it inadvertently and where children will not come across it at all unless their parents or some other adult allows them to do so. (That is the objective of the law: obviously there will always be leakage.)

Can one bring this about on something like the Internet? The solution cannot lie in barring access to Internet for children for apart from practicalities, there are going to be many things on the Internet that will be of interest and value to children. So there will have to be controls over access to sections of what is available on the Internet. This is a technical and economic problem to which I do not have a solution. However, I do have one encouraging thought. It seems to me in general that we should cheer up (as Adam Smith would remind us) if the requirements of general social policy and morality coincide with the motives of profit. There are strong motives for people to devise ways of constraining access to the Internet for consumers and to provide a reward for publishers on it. So there will be devices for controlling access to particular sectors or programmes or databases on the Internet, and these can be mobilised to help us with this problem as well.

There is a last subject I would like to take up, because it is a matter of some concern to me. One of the things that we did not deal with adequately in our report, because we did not foresee them, were of course these more recent technological developments, including even the widespread circulation of videos. But there has also been a cultural development. We did not adequately address what would now be identified as among the principal objections to pornography, those from a feminist perspective. This was not altogether our fault, as a matter of fact; we sent out an appeal in the middle of our enquiry, saying that we would like to hear more of women's opinions on this subject, and we got practically nothing in reply. That would not be the case now.

I shall say one or two things about this subject, and I am sorry if because of the shortage of time they sound rather dogmatic. The first point is that everybody, feminists and others, must not forget that the aim of a discussion such as that in our Report is to formulate a law. Even if we agree that certain material is offensive to women or even damaging to their interests, the question remains of how one gets those considerations into a court of law. Ultimately, someone has to be able to get up and say in a non-arbitrary manner that beyond reasonable doubt, or by some similar standard, a given work offends against the law. The best-known proposals for a legal provision in feminist terms, those made by Catherine Mackinnon and Andrea Dworkin, are in fact, though this is often forgotten, for a civil offence: they set out grounds for bringing an action against a publisher. Indeed, Professor Mackinnon agreed with me in a television discussion (though, unfortunately, in a part of the programme which the BBC did not eventually transmit) that so far as her proposals went she had no reason to support the British Obscene Publications Act, and that she did not believe in the state operating a criminal offence in this area. But whether as a civil or a criminal matter, the point is that feminist provisions against pornography must be "justiciable".

Next we have to ask what the motivation is for having such a law. It is a pity that some feminists (by no means all) have endorsed an old-fashioned positivist approach to this subject, which treats provisions about pornography as a branch of public health legislation. The model is that of controlling a noxious substance which causes certain specific and statistically recognisable harms. In the preamble to the Minnesota Ordnance that was advanced by Mackinnon and Dworkin, there are vast and reckless claims to the effect that pornography is known to be the cause of rape, sexual crime, child abuse and other evils. As propositions of social science, I do not believe that such claims are any better substantiated now than they were when we examined them in 1977–79. I am not denying – on the contrary – that there is an extremely important feminist contribution to the critique and understanding of pornography. I merely want to deny that this contribution best takes the form of entering an outmoded and unilluminating debate about the statistical effects of pornography.

I shall end with four last observations on the feminist issue. The first is simply that it is worth bearing in mind that not all pornography is about women: there is such a thing as male gay pornography. Secondly, as some feminists have pointed out (Erica Jong has mentioned some of them, and similar points have been made, for instance, by Linda Williams in her book *Hardcore*) – pornography can play a liberating role with respect to sexism. In that connection, thirdly, there is a simple point to be made.

It is often assumed in these debates that since a great deal of pornography is sexist, hard-core pornography must be more sexist than soft-core pornography. That is simply a mistake. A lot of hard-core pornography, of course, is exceedingly sexist, but much of it is not. This is for the simple reason that the definition of the difference between hard-core pornography and soft-core pornography is itself sexist: hard-core pornography is that in which penetration and the erect penis are displayed, while soft-core pornography is that in which women are seen aroused and men are not. Some soft-core pornography, such as the well-known and widely distributed movie Emmanuelle, consists of naked women embracing one another or masturbating or writhing or whatever, being watched by clothed men in suits (who, to make things worse, exchange pseudo-Gallic worldly wisdom about life and love). Such movies were not, of course, the most revolting or affronting examples of pornography that I witnessed in the course of my long and trying career in this subject, but they were among the most sexist. It is a serious point that much hard-core pornography represents the sexuality of women and men equally, and this, by definition, is not true of soft-core pornography.

My last point is general and political. One feminist, a friend of mine with whom I had a debate on this subject in Berkeley, started her remarks on that occasion by saying "I shall omit the views of religious fundamentalists and reactionary political figures". I said to her, "I'm afraid you can't omit the views of religious fundamentalists and reactionary political figures, because what you want to propose is also proposed by those figures." I could have gone on to say "In supporting the same cause, you cannot dismiss the point that the proposals of the religious fundamentalists and reactionary political figures would have consequences harmful to the interests of women. Feminism is not itself a popular cause with many who want to suppress or otherwise constrain pornography, and if you are very concerned with women's freedom and the expressions that go with that and, indeed, with free discussion of women's sexuality, it's not enormously wise to get on the same bus as people who want none of this." The old saying is that "you need a long spoon to sup with the devil". It is just as true that you need a long spoon to sup with the righteous.

PAGE THREE, INDECENT DISPLAY AND THE ROOTS OF CONCERN

Clare Short MP

I was sitting in the House of Commons one Friday, when I would rather have been in Birmingham, when Winston Churchill"s "laundry list" Bill was on. It was a Mary Whitehouse bill, which proposed a list of visual images that should always be obscene. It was a ridiculous and outrageous bill, which would have outlawed most war reporting. I remember we had letters from people, who provided sex education to young people with learning disabilities, saying it would have outlawed the pictures that they used.

However, I wasn't there because of that bill, but because the next bill was Enoch Powell's bill to outlaw any embryo research which would have made illegal any help to couples with infertility problems. Jo Richardson and I were there. As you know, one of the ways you prevent something becoming law is to talk at great length on something entirely different. So we had to keep the discussion going on the Winston Churchill bill, to stop the Enoch Powell bill getting to a vote, as we didn't have enough people there to ensure it was defeated.

I heard a series of speeches about how women in Britain were deeply concerned about rape and sexual assault and how the people of Britain, particularly the women of Britain, would never forgive the House of Commons if we didn't pass this bill. I had no intention of speaking that day, I had no written speech, I was just there in case I was needed. But I became more and more irritated by these arguments, and I got up and made a short, unscripted speech saying what an absolute danger to liberty this bill was, how unprincipled and ridiculous the thinking behind it was.

I also said that I agreed that there were lots of women in Britain who were outraged by both the levels of pornography that circulated in our society and the degree of sexual crime and rape, and that my own view was that one of the things that we could do to push back the tide was to remove the Page 3 phenomenon from our newspapers. I said I thought it didn't belong there, that newspapers circulating on buses and sitting on kitchen tables shouldn't have pornographic images of women within them. We have in our law a principle (which Bernard Williams has enlarged on in his very useful and interesting analysis), which is that things which are legal in magazines you might buy and take home cannot be on hoardings in the street, that we have some right to be protected from things bearing down on us without our consent, and that the only alternative isn't absolute illegality: there is a space in between which seeks to restrict the circulation of such images.

There is a law called the Indecent Displays Act that entrenches in law this principle, and I was simply trying to extend that principle to newspapers, so that we could wipe out this phenomenon of half-naked women in our newspapers. As I got carried along in my little speech, I said, "In fact I think I might introduce my own Bill on this". I sat down and thought now I'll have to do it.

So I went away and did a little bit of work and applied for my slot for a ten-minute rule bill and introduced my bill. What followed was extraordinary. First there was all the misbehaviour of men in the House of Commons on the day, because so many of them are so unrepresentative that if you mention cervical cancer or breasts or whatever, half of them fall on the floor and giggle. (This is the reason why I find it so offensive that people question our commitment to the selection of more women MPs on the grounds that it will not constitute selection by merit!) Then there was also a big media reaction sneering at me in a similar way to some of the men in the House of Commons. And thirdly there was a phenomenal reaction from women in Britain. I received 10,000–15,000 letters, passionate letters, from women up and down this land saying things like "I'm not a feminist, or I didn't think I was, but I've hated all this stuff all my life and I've never dared to say so because everyone said I was screwed up, and it's so wonderful to know other people think like me – thank you, thank you, thank you".

These women were pouring out views that no-one had given any legitimacy to. There were letters from women who had been sexually abused as children who said that every time they were confronted by that kind of material it distressed them and reminded them, and that sometimes such material was used in the course of the abuse, and so on. Lots of women who breast-fed their children contrasted a society that humiliated them because they chose to look for somewhere to breast-feed their child, and yet bombarded them with images of breast, but when the breast was used for its natural purpose it was seen as filthy and dirty and they had to go and do it in the toilet. Letters from women who were receiving psychiatric treatment because they were told they were so peculiar because they objected to pornography. There was an absolute tide, and the emotion of it.

You can't ignore such a powerful, passionate, moving voice that no-one was organising – this was no campaign, this was just women up and down Britain writing these eloquent, moving and powerful letters. Then there was a little bit somewhere in a *Guardian* diary item saying that I'd received lots of letters from women. Then I got hundreds of letters from men apologising profusely for not having written before, that they didn't realise that it was only women that were writing and they actually hated pornography too. Lots of decent, detailed letters of a different kind, seeing it as degrading to them and their sexuality but not quite as personal, as hurt and as passionate as the letters from women.

That was my experience from individual citizens on the one hand. On the other hand, a number of Murdoch papers and others, set out to silence and to try to destroy me. Here am I, one little Labour MP saying in a ten-minute speech in the House of Commons that I think the principles in the Indecent Displays Act should be extended to newspapers. This is a simple proposition, we can all think about it and talk about it and decide whether we agree or not. But the vehemence of the attack on me was deeply irrational.

There was something more going on than a rational proposal to be discussed about where we draw our legislative lines. There were constant knocking stories, and they couldn't decide what to do with me, I was either a sort of vile, man-hating, joyless, probably lesbian woman, or the following week I was a floosie. The images changed, but the attacks just came constantly and they were powerful and irrational. *The News of the World* then put a lot of resources into crawling through my life since I was 16 years old, trying to find anyone that I had ever had any friendship or relationship with, finding a former husband who was offered lots of money to try and damage me.

I think that the passion, emotion and irrationality of the attacks on me demonstrate the strength of the feminist critique of pornography. Part of the reason for the emotion is that it goes right to the heart of what women are seeking in sexual relationships. Most women are seeking a mutuality and a mutual respect around sexuality and find the separation of sex from emotion quite frightening. They fear a culture of masculinity that seeks to separate sex from relationships. The pornography industry in Britain is, I'm told, bigger than the whole of our film and music industry combined. I think that when we look at what our culture is and we look at those figures, this is deeply depressing. It's also true that in our country and across the world the prostitution industry is massive. So there are lots and lots of men consuming pornography that separates depictions of women and their availability to be used and disposed of from any relationship with any real woman, and prostitution is another version of that sexuality without relationship.

I suspect that at the core of the emotion around all of this is a view of sexuality that women feel terribly threatened by, are aware of all the hurt that comes from that difference. For example, one in four violent crimes in Britain arises from domestic violence, and many women feel that stopping pornography is like getting rid of all that hurt and harm, pushing it away, saying no to it. My own view is that it's massively important to have the discussion about what pornography is about, who is it for, who consumes it. We should consider the very interesting and important distinction between soft pornography that is supposedly all right but constantly shows the woman as there to be used, disposed of and thrown away, and hard-core pornography that depicts normal acts of sexual intercourse and also lots of violence and sadomasochism and Nazi regalia and all sorts of horrible add-ons that degrade sexuality in the way that women find so frightening.

I think it's important to have that discussion quite apart from, and separate from, any question of legislative proposals. It is liberating in itself for some of those thousands of women to find out that other women feel like them, that they're not screwed up about sex because they hate pornography, that we're allowed to talk about what we think is lovely about sex and what we think is horrible about it. I think that debate enlarges freedom, and that there are an awful lot of forces with vested interests who want to silence the debate. I think it was symbolised in the attacks on me and the attempt to silence me. There was no prospect of the bill being passed. Yet the impact of such a small amount of Parliamentary time was remarkable. The debate rumbled around the country, households throughout the land had the discussion. There is clearly something there, rich and passionate, that people want to talk about and are entitled to talk about and that it's liberating for women to be able to talk about.

As a consequence of that experience I also think that we are very very foolish, those of us who count ourselves to be liberals, those of us who need and care for freedom of speech and freedom of thought and freedom of the arts, if we don't attend to this debate. If we say "Oh no, we're liberals, anything goes, we have nothing to say, we are silent on this," then along comes Mrs Whitehouse and everything she represented and some of the other terribly reactionary forces that exist in the United States of America, to misuse the emotions of this debate for their own ends. Mrs Whitehouse represents the tradition that says sex is vile and ugly and it's better if you don't do it, but if you have to do it it should be within marriage and for procreation only. This is the "better to marry than burn" tradition which is a deep part, of course, of our cultural and historical tradition.

Mrs Whitehouse also said the Vietnam War should not have been reported in the way it was because those pictures and that reporting undermined the will of American youth to fight, and she also said something similar about the war in Namibia in relation to South African young people. There is a passionate and strongly-held view, among women predominantly but also among quite a lot of men, that objects to pornography for reasons around aspirations to human dignity and fineness. This needs addressing and respecting, otherwise the emotions that flow around – and they're very powerful emotions – are dragged into the right wing's hands and can be misused for an agenda that uses these passions to legitimise very dangerous political censorship. I profoundly disagree with those who say if you make any restriction you legitimise censorship therefore you can't control anything, therefore anything goes, because then you give the whole of this to the right in a most dangerous way. That is the second of my very strongly-held conclusions.

Thirdly, I think that the way this argument is often posed and, to an extent, a lot of what Erica Jong argues, is on a most naïve and extraordinary level. It is as if we have two worlds – one is called freedom and the other is when some people like me come along and propose some censorship. Such an argument rests on the assumption that if Mr Murdoch and whoever else might monopolise our media outlets do exactly what they want and publish exactly what they want, and distribute exactly what they want, that is freedom. For example, I believe it is an abuse of power that the revolting *Sunday Sport* and top-shelf magazines are circulated by monopoly distributors to all local newsagents who have to take them if they want newspapers. There are lots of local newsagents who do not want to carry this material, but if they say so, they are not allowed to sell newspapers which threatens their business. So this isn't an expression of freedom, this is a powerful monopoly at work.

I think it says something really very strong about our culture that in the corner shops that children probably take most interest in, where comics and sweets are sold, there is a *Sunday Sport* and a barrage of magazines that you can see on the top shelf depicting a pornographic image of women and sexuality. I think that is extraordinary. I think it says something deep about our culture. It's reasonable to say this material can be available for those who seek it out, but it should not beam down on those of us who don't want it and it should not, in particular, beam down at children in the places they go to buy the goodies of their life.

So I am arguing that there is no such thing as censorship or not censorship. There are going to be some who own our media outlets, some who decide what is portrayed, and we have to decide whether we allow concentrations of media ownership, whether we have public service broadcasting, whether we require programming aimed at children, how much religious broadcasting, where do we draw the lines, because everyone who commissions a play about sexuality, love, passion or any hurt, will have to draw some lines about how that is depicted and what is tasteful and what is not. So all the time there are people making these judgements. We have to make the judgements. It's an unavoidable discussion. There is no such thing as the freedom people on one side and then some other horrible censorship people on the other. Being a human being means that you are part of this discussion: having standards and taste is part of being a human being.

Having said that we have, of course, to carry on and re-regulate and look at the changes in new forms of media and whether we allow cross-media ownership between press and television. None of these questions are ever answered for all time, they are part of the questions of what is our culture and what is our taste. So when we admit that these are questions that are unavoidable and that everyone must engage with, we then have to say it's all a question of who draws the lines and where they are drawn, and how can we do this as well as possible to enlarge what is good and to allow freedom to all who want to experiment.

I think first of all we have to admit that child pornography is absolutely objectionable and it should always be restricted and should always be a criminal offence. It goes further than what Bernard advocated this morning. The police who work in this area tell us that whenever you find child pornography you find paedophilia and they chase child pornography in order to find rings of paedophiles who are sexually abusing children.

There is room for an argument about whether we should control adult pornography. Clearly child pornography is in a totally different category and I think there is hardly any human being in our society who would say there should be no restrictions of any kind around that. In our country we have a law that says it's an offence to incite racial hatred – we should have that law, it's about decency, it's about not allowing some people to be belittled and humiliated by racist comments and racist depictions of Jewish people or black people as inferior. I think it's an enlargement of freedom to have that law. We must recognise that this law is part of this whole debate.

I am also sure that the overwhelming majority of people think that we should have categories for our films about what kind of film is suitable for what kind of people. Clearly, we overwhelmingly agree that there's some material, some levels of gratuitous violence and violent sexual arousal, that we believe should not be given a licence and therefore not allowed in mainstream cinema. But some of those films could be shown in clubs, but not shown in mainstream cinemas, and I think most people would agree with that.

Then there is the question of how you categorise what is suitable for children, what is suitable for adults, and what is suitable for parental guidance. We might have to argue about who does it, who appoints the boards, have they got the principles right. We should also address what the principles should be, what kind of depiction of women should have. Maybe, we should also have more women on the board.

I think virtually everyone agrees that we have to have some categorisation. After the recent argument about whether videos that were very gratuitously violent could be hired out to children, we tightened the law. I strongly supported this change. I like the fact that those who try to – it's the forces of the market again – make money out of hiring out videos to children have to look again at the level of violence because if they don't get their licence they won't make as much money. There is, of course, a question of what is gratuitous violence, who makes the judgements. But I think these are reasonable questions and most people in Britain think we should draw such lines.

I think that all of these questions are unavoidable. The pretence that there is something called freedom or some odd people that want something called censorship is a complete confusion and does not take anyone forward and is not a description of reality. What is very important is firstly that we frame the principles that we wish to apply, and the principle, it seems to me, is that some things are so vile they are not permitted. This is why I'm so interested in what Bernard Williams has to say about pornography that depicts something that would be illegal in reality. It might not fully deal with the question of child pornography, but it's a very useful starting point. So some things, then, would always be illegal and always prosecuted. You would not catch it all, but that is not the point; you do not catch all murderers but no-one says that therefore we should cease to make murder a criminal offence.

Much more complicated is the question of that material which is deeply and passionately offensive to lots of women and damaging to children, but which lots of men want to consume and want to spend lots of money on. That's where the really hard question arises. I think the principle behind the Indecent Displays Act and the principle that I was putting forward about the Page 3 phenomenon is that that kind of material can be made available for those who seek it out, but it must not be displayed to and imposed on those who do not want it. Underpinning that is a judgement that it is undesirable and offensive. You could rest on the principle that it is simply offensive, but I go back to what I call the feminist analysis of pornography, that it is offensive, that it is degrading, that it does degrade human sexuality. That is my judgement. I accept that there are many men who want this kind of material. I think it's one of our problems and I think it's one of the reasons why men and women hurt each other so often, but that is a slightly different discussion. My conclusion is that such material must be kept in a separate place, never displayed, never imposed; it can be bought and read in private but not imposed on those of us who do not want it.

When we look at new media outlets such as the Internet, we should separate getting the principles right and the technical difficulties of applying those principles to a new outlet. It's very important not to jumble up those arguments and say, oh dear, we've got the Internet, there's nothing we can do about it. I think there are suggestions of libel actions involving the Internet, involving copyright and libel which will start to create rules. How people are going to work this out technically, I don't know, but I'm sure it can be done. If we can frame what we require according to our principles, then we can say to those who know "Help us with this, we're trying to apply these principles", in order to preserve freedom and decency.

A jungle ruled by the free market is ugly and debases humanity. The suggestion that the free market in porn or in gratuitous violence is freedom and that people like us trying to use the limited power of democracy to impose some restrictions and principles on these media barons is censorship, seems to me to distort the meaning of language. Everything that is fine and precious needs nurturing and protecting. Any culture that celebrates unrestricted freedom for pornography and gratuitous violence is destroying itself.

FREE AND FAIR COMMUNICATION AND THE REGULATION OF MEDIA CONTENT

Michael Grade

Broadcasting regulation in the UK over the past 50 years has been based on three significant factors. The first is that broadcasting has been a highly restricted activity, government-licensed, with very few players compared with other forms of mass communication. Starting as a state monopoly in the 1920s, the pace of expansion was very slow indeed. In television the monopoly ended with the establishment of ITV in 1955. A third channel (BBC2) was added in the following decade, and the fourth (Channel 4) not until 1982. The limits of technology – spectrum shortage in the jargon – made television a very special activity indeed.

The second factor shaping the regulatory environment has been the almost universal perception that television is a uniquely influential medium. Politicians in particular have tended to view it as a powerful, mind-changing medium. They have sought both to use it, and to curb it, according to this sometimes over-exaggerated belief. And they are quick, too quick, to blame television for a whole catalogue of social ills from the distressing triviality of popular culture through to the rising crime rate. Somehow blaming the box in the corner gives them a fleeting absolution from any guilt they may feel about their impotence in the face of the intractability of society's ills.

And thirdly, combining the fact of restricted access to television with its perceived social and political impact, it has been viewed generally as a medium quite different in kind to print. It is therefore deemed to need a much greater degree of regulation. Unlike print, its operation is not simply left to the laws of the land. Extra rules and structures have been deemed appropriate to achieve impartiality, and to monitor standards of "taste and decency". If we look at the performance of regulation against its objectives over the past half century, we find both the good and the bad, elements of real success mixed with less palatable results.

In terms of impartiality, it has been something of a triumph, though not, as any politician or broadcasters will tell you, without bad temper and bitter battles. British television is as neutral and unbiased as you could expect any human activity to be. Yes, there are mistakes, and sometimes very bad ones. But – like plane crashes – they are the mistakes that illustrate by their rarity how effectively the system normally runs.

The press, of course, runs on different tracks. Print escaped from government control in the 18th and 19th centuries and has fully exercised its democratic right to editorialise in the 20th century. A free press is held to be a vital symbol of democracy, even when, as in this country, it has resulted overall in a right-of-centre bias. No one suggests altering that. But compare it with the effective neutrality of broadcasting, which has been built on the early foundations laid by the BBC, and which is widely recognised as valuable and necessary in a mature democracy. Some of the legislative attempts to prescribe impartiality in greater detail have of course been risible, but the principle is sound. It isn't seen as censorship, but public welfare. It is an interesting and probably a necessary paradox that the freedom to editorialise in print is essential to free speech, whilst the requirement for television to be unbiased is a necessary service to democracy.

The regulation of taste and decency has, however, always been a much more difficult and contentious area. Let me make clear that in this instance I'm not talking about the outer fringes of exploitation and pornography, or the demeaning and dehumanising material which all but the most debased minds would reject out of hand. The problem lies in the middle ground. It is easy to legislate, but words are ill defined, the debate is confused, and subjective opinions and emotions almost always overwhelm such objective facts as may be available. Just whose taste and decency are we talking about? Who should we appoint to make these judgements? What powers should we give them? How can we believe that anyone is uniquely skilled to make these close calls, to remain themselves uncorrupted as they protect us from corruption?

Clearly, there are specific needs. There is, above all, the need to protect children. All broadcasters accept, and abide by the concept of the watershed. That can be defined, and prescriptively applied. But the danger is of the application of white, largely male, middle-class, middle-aged tastes to a mass medium which seeks to inform and entertain a much wider and more diverse public. History is littered with examples of great works which were thought offensive to conventional good taste on their first outings – Rodin's *The Kiss* – Stravinsky's *Rite of Spring* or Monty Python. Of course not all television – or indeed very much of it – is art in that sense. But it has become the main creative engine of popular culture, and will frequently want to test conventions and break boundaries. Is that really so dangerous? Isn't there an opposite – and who knows, greater – danger in artificially constraining that creativity by not trusting the broadcasters' knowledge of both their producers and their audiences?

A balance must clearly be struck between creative liberty and unbridled licence. It is one of the central conundrums of a mass medium. Should the rules and conventions which govern content be framed to satisfy a simple majority of the population? Or should they prevent broadcasters from risking offence to the most sensitive 10 per cent of viewers? If so, you might as well argue that all swimming pools should be no more than three feet deep, because a tenth of the population can't swim. And in the end, if the broadcasters can't be trusted to get the balance right, what chance have small groups of arbitrarily and generally appointed regulators?

It is not a problem with an easy answer, and it is made no easier by the haphazard structure of overlapping regulatory authorities which has grown up in Britain, and by the arcane manner in which appointments to them are made. In commercial television, I am currently answerable to the Independent Television Commission, the Broadcasting Standards Council and the Broadcasting Complaints Commission. At least they are separate and external to me. The BBC has the difficulty that the Governors in law are the Corporation, and thus are its publisher. Yet they – another collection of non-professional broadcasters – are also deemed to act effectively as its external regulator. Perhaps that peculiarity is what leads to extraordinary decisions like the postponing of two Panorama programmes for no other apparent reason than the fact that they were embarrassing to the government. Funny how regulation in Britain always defines the public interest as preventing publication – never in ensuring it, never once.

When I visited South Africa to give evidence to the new broadcasting commission, I was very impressed by the open and democratic way in which this regulatory body had been established. The selection process was supervised by the judiciary, following clear legislative guidelines, appointing the best candidates from the literally thousands of nominees who responded to a public invitation to apply. The members thus selected are well-informed, intelligent, and above all are collectively fully in touch with the needs, interests and aspirations of the whole population of their culturally diverse country. They are external to the broadcasting organisations, but professionally alert to their purposes and problems. Above all they seem able to take a wide view of their society at large.

I have no doubt that our own regulators have worked hard to make the best of their disparate briefs, but I can't help thinking how much better it would be if they, too, were more democratically selected, and if their attitude to broadcasting were a little less driven by the need to prevent minor transgressions of their own particular cultural standards. Do we really need regulators to act like medieval schoolmen, determining just which swear words are permissible, and at just which hour before midnight? Do we really need apparently learned treatises on violence which include news coverage of earthquakes in that category? That said, we have survived our first 50 years with, on the whole not many casualties of censorship, little palpable evidence of damage to the body politic, a satisfied public, a vigorous production industry, generally high standards, and an enviable body of experienced broadcasters. The challenge now is the transition to a rapidly changing future.

All the main factors which have shaped our present system will be called into question by the technological developments which lie ahead. The impact of an ever-growing number of channels will make itself felt. It will be much more difficult for regulators to be proactive when there is simply too much output for them and their officials to watch. The Radio Authority has reached that point already, now relying increasingly on audience complaints before they can act. It may be much longer before television reaches the same point – especially given that the existing terrestrial channels will hold a very substantial share of viewing for many years to come – but, eventually, it will impossible for regulation to continue in its present proactive, interventionist form.

The second change will also be gradual, and also inexorable. Currently, government interest is focussed on the regulation of cross-media ownership. We all assume – probably rightly – that the different editorial expectations of print and screen can be maintained for the foreseeable future. Even so, even in the much shorter term, do not underestimate the editorial power available to cross-media owners through the cross-promotion of their new broadcasting services in their newspaper titles. How is that commercial power be dealt with?

However, I do have a niggling doubt whether the distinctions between print and screen can endure forever. As I have indicated, in a multi-channel future, how closely will every new service be policed? If there were to be a thousand channels, why shouldn't they begin to differentiate themselves according to political or religious persuasion? And just what constitutes broadcasting? What about that new devil, convergence, with the Telegraph and other papers now available on-line? What is the boundary between computing, telephony and broadcasting?

It is just too easy to say that technology will provide enough channels of distribution to free television from the shackles of neutrality, and let a thousand flowers bloom. It would certainly mark an end to the supposed "censorship" of the current impartiality requirement, but would it benefit the public, would it benefit the democratic system. We are all free to start a newspaper now, but very few of us have deep enough pockets to do so. Access to the printer on the corner is no substitute for the power of distributing a national newspaper. It's the old market freedom of the sharks to eat the minnows.

In broadcasting, the scale is even greater, and will remain high even after all the new opportunities of cable and local television are in place. The cost of entry for mass television is huge, and so is the ongoing cost of production. Do not be misled by the seductive promise of the super-highway. Most viewing will remain dominated by the great corporations, with major stakes in both production and distribution. Can we also allow them to set our agendas in terms of news and information? Ten years from now I believe that this will become a major issue. I have no magic solution, other than to suggest that we might see multi-level regulation, with stricter rules for bigger mass audience television services, and increasing freedom to publish for new forms of electronic publishing. And that would doubtless call for a new regulator with the judgement of Solomon, and with eyes in the back of his/her head!

The impact of channel expansion on taste and decency follows something of the same pattern. Again, multiple channels will be harder to monitor, but even more important factors will be at work. A division is clearly growing between channels whose primary purpose is public service (in the widest sense), and those which are obviously businesses seeking to maximise profits. For the former (in the UK, the BBC and Channel 4) the ambition is to succeed in innovation, in refreshing the pool of home grown programmes, and in accurately reflecting and stimulating the public mood and taste. Conflicts over censorship and regulation, tensions between liberty and licence will continue with ongoing debate over creative freedoms, imposed conservatism and the fear of the new. And there will always be mistakes: television sometimes gets it quite wrong.

Fully commercial channels, on the other hand, are innovating less and less, here and elsewhere. They are less and less likely to shock or offend established culture through novelty or unfamiliarity. The danger for them is the temptation to push the boundaries of exploitation, with the dreary and over-repeated use of sex and violence in culturally valueless and derivative formats, with the sole purpose of selling airtime. Regulation will never make for high art, but it has a continuing role in ensuring – as far as it can – that truly damaging and exploitative material is kept to an absolute minimum. As with the impartiality question I have no simple solution. Indeed, it is much easier and attractive to regulators to leap in and condemn a couple of expletives in a one-off play, especially created for the British audience, than it is to deal with the ongoing levels of sexual exploitation and the tolerance of unnecessary violence which are threatening to become part and parcel of the lower strata of popular entertainment.

Perhaps in the end such problems are insoluble. Perhaps there is no practicable and credible means of drawing boundaries other than those set in statute law, and even then proof is a contentious matter. Perhaps in a democracy freedom to publish must take precedence over any cultural sensibilities. And perhaps the best medicine is to make sure that the public service broadcasters, those who put the public interest first, those who are committed to sustaining a creative, non-derivative production base, are properly supported, properly sustained, and properly funded.

This is a timely moment to discuss the complex issues of how best to regulate broadcasting as it moves into an exciting but uncertain future. There are many issues to cover, and many debates to be had as the plot unfolds. If I can make one final plea it is this. Technology is always fascinating, and we are all at times dazzled by the promises it holds. Rightly so, for it is the technology which empowers us to carry on our trade, and to make it better. But please, let us not fall into the trap of believing that progress is cost-free, or even problem-free, or that technology provides its own answers to the difficulties it often presents. I ask you to keep clear in your minds the purposes of broadcasting, and not be side-tracked by its methods. In the end, the public interest will remain very much the same as it is now: a right to free and fair communication, to choice, to unbiased news, and to enjoy the highest standard of output – in all genres – that our native talent can produce.

FREEDOM AND LIMITS IN EXPRESSION

Chris Smith MP

About ten or eleven years ago, Customs and Excise raided Gay's the Word bookshop in Camden, north London, and took away a hefty pile of material which had been imported from both Europe and the United States, including selected works by Oscar Wilde, E. M. Forster and Radclyffe Hall, as being in contravention of the Customs Consolidation Act of 1890. When questioned in court about on what grounds they had made these decisions, the reply from the Customs' officers in court was, "Well, all of these works are about homosexuals, so they must be in contravention of the Customs Act mustn't they?"

I think that the best parliamentary question which was subsequently tabled was from my colleague Frank Dobson, whose constituency the bookshop was in. He asked what had been the amount of police resources in time and money in carrying out the raid and then in subsequently reading the material seized. The answer to the second part of the question was that this information was not available centrally and would be too expensive to provide. So I start with a prejudice in favour of free expression and I think the fundamental starting point of any discussion on expression, freedom of speech, what rules and regulations there can and should be, has to be that the presumption must always be in favour of free expression, but, and it's a big but, there is a line to be drawn I believe to prevent liberty becoming licence or exploitation.

Now in some cases the drawing of that line is fairly obvious. Let's take something which is I believe a very clear example and that is the prevention of incitement to racial hatred. We have laws on the statute book in this country which say that you cannot either in print or in speech incite to racial hatred. Absolutely right that we should have such rules but that is a circumscription on freedom of speech, and we have to recognise that in trying to balance these two objectives the law has, in my view rightly, decided that there must be some degree of restriction. The exploitation of children or women or minorities are other examples where the law has, I believe, a right to say there are boundaries beyond which freedom of expression cannot go, but it is the decisions about where you draw those lines and how you set about drawing them and on what principles you draw them and who decides where they should be drawn, it is those issues that I believe are the crucial and difficult ones and, in many cases, impossible to define in a blanket way.

I would give as one example the role of the depiction of violence on television. Now I have to say I am considerably more worried about the effect of violence on viewers than I am about the effect of the depiction of sexual encounters on viewers, but let's just look for a moment at the depiction of violence. You may have an extremely violent scene taking place which produces shock and horror and disgust in the viewers on the one hand, and on the other hand you may have a scene which is violent but portrays what I would describe as sanitised violence. An example that might serve would be some episodes of "The A Team" where an enormous amount of violence goes on but no one gets hurt. Now which, I ask you, is actually the more serious in terms of its effect on the viewer. Is it the violence which is cruel and nasty and horrible and induces revulsion and is designed to induce revulsion in the viewer, or is it the violence that somehow comes across as not mattering? I would argue that actually the second of those categories is probably far more damaging in its effect than the first, and yet how on earth can we define laws which say that form of violence is not acceptable and something else is acceptable: it is very difficult to make those distinctions.

I suppose the first general point that I would want to make is that while we must start with the presumption in favour of free expression, while we must recognise that there are clearly some limits that can be placed and should be placed on that, at the same time we also have to recognise the enormous difficulty of determining precisely where those limits should lie. Now this dilemma leads me on to my second point which is to tread delicately into the debate that has been raging for a while about individuals' right to privacy from media intrusion, because exactly the same difficulties of drawing boundaries applies here. I think most sensible people would probably say that if you are an ordinary individual, not seeking the public limelight in any way, then you should be entitled to a certain amount of privacy. If, on the other hand, you are a public figure and it is in the public interest for something that you are up to become known widely and generally, then there is a right for intrusion of privacy to take place. But let me give you two examples. Mrs Brown of 123 Acacia

Avenue, who is an entirely private citizen, has not sought the public limelight in any way at all, gives birth to quins; immediately she becomes a person of public interest. Does that mean that journalists are then entitled to intrude upon her privacy in order to report her circumstances to the world?

I am not sure of the answer to that question. On the other hand, Russell Harty was undoubtedly a public figure, of enormous public interest, but I do not believe for a moment that entitled journalists to enter his hotel bedroom when he was on his deathbed to take pictures. There are grey areas where there are clearly some important principles at stake, but how you apply those principles to the nitty gritty of real life circumstances becomes extremely difficult. My answer to the privacy dilemma is to enshrine the European Convention on Human Rights into UK law in a bill of rights, which includes a right to individual privacy and a right to free expression. At the same time, it ensures that there are two other things on the statute book. One is a clear defence of acting in the public interest for journalistic practice and the other is to ensure that there is proper freedom of information legislation about governmental activity on the statute book. With that framework in place, of a right to privacy, a right to free expression, a defence of public interest and freedom of information, then the courts must carry out the job of determining in any one particular case how those different principles intermesh, because I do not think you can prescribe for every eventuality predictively in law.

That brings me on to the existing rules about broadcasting and the press and how they effectively work and attached to that the various bodies that stand as guardians and regulator. We know that the government is in the process of merging the Broadcasting Standards Council and the Broadcasting Complaints Commission, and we're in favour of that because anything that gets rid of overlapping bureaucracy is worth doing. However, that still leaves us with a great gallery of different bodies carrying out regulatory functions with varying degrees of accountability. Let me just take one of them, the Board of Governors of the BBC. Michael Grade has quite rightly identified the dilemma that the Board of Governors are the BBC but that they are also the BBC's regulators. To a certain extent, with an institution that is formed under Royal Charter, that is the public service broadcaster par excellence, and to a certain extent you can't get away from that dilemma. But what we can do surely is to make the

Governors rather more accountable for what they do. I know the IPPR have come up with some alternative suggestions in their paper *The Future of the BBC*, but just to throw into the debate, I would suggest another mechanism for a degree of greater accountability.

Why don't we make appointments to the BBC Board of Governors subject to ratification and interview by the Select Committee on Heritage in the House of Commons? Why don't we also have a system where instead of the government appointing the chairman of the Board of Governors, the governors themselves choose their own chairman, and why don't we in addition to that, insist that the governors present a report every year to the select committee on their work as governors, completely separate from the BBC's annual report? In that way we would at least begin to get a little more openness and accountability into the way in which the Board of Governors operates, and then perhaps we can start looking at some of the other bodies and getting a greater amount of transparency into their work as well. One other factor is that so long as you have a system of franchising of commercial television stations, both for Channel 3 and now for Channel 5, that depends primarily on price in determining who gets the franchise, then the quality of content is always going to come second in consideration. That, inevitably, has a knock on effect into the type of broadcasting which people receive and that's why we would want to change the system of allocating franchises so that quality comes above price in the determination of who gets the franchise. I was interested to hear that British Telecom was talking about the "old-fashioned" Internet. Well yes, it is actually quite old-fashioned, it's horrendously slow, especially if you're trying to gain access to it when both Britain and America are at work, and it will change dramatically as new broadband communication links gradually become established.

The development of these new networks will undoubtedly bring about massive changes in the way in which we interact, the way in which we exchange information, the way in which we receive broadcast entertainment. I very much want to see put in place an open-access principle for the new networks, so that simply because someone happens to own the infrastructure, or a portion of the infrastructure, should not mean that they can dictate what can and can't go along it. Now if you have an open-access principle so that the provider of any material or any service should have access to the new interactive broadband networks, then immediately a question follows. Should you then say that there are some things which cannot and should not go along the new networks. I would argue that the answer to that must be yes. If it is wrong to incite to racial hatred on the town-hall steps or in a broadsheet that you put round people's doorsteps, it must be wrong to incite to racial hatred across the new electronic media.

We should ensure that our various laws also apply to electronic forms of communication. Of course, there are problems because anyone can put any information onto the electronic media from anywhere. You can perhaps stop this, as in the University of Michigan case where someone who has put on a particular amount of material is identified by the authorities in the country where they have done it and there are laws on the statue book. In such a case, an individual can be taken to court, no problem.

But, what happens if someone is sitting in Colombia or Guatemala or Romania and putting material onto the international communication networks, which is then received by people in Britain and there are no reciprocal laws between Britain and the country of origin about what material can and can't be passed along the networks? You immediately have a problem. That is why I would argue that we need some pretty urgent international discussions about the flow of information across the new networks. If we can have laws of the sea and laws of outer space, surely it shouldn't be a total impossibility to achieve a network of laws of cyberspace.

So far so good. You have crossed the first hurdle, which is to put the existing body of law into applicability to electronic media. You have then sought international agreement between different countries to ensure that you cover wherever the material is coming from, But what if the material has been put on entirely anonymously, so the originator of the material cannot be identified? I have to confess, I don't have an answer to that problem. You could conceivably require that in the systems everyone should have a digital signature that carries their imprimatur with any piece of information that they put onto the network, but I think that would probably be too intrusive. It does mean, however, that we end up having a problem about the anonymous provision of information. There are ways in which we could think about attacking this problem, but I don't have a perfect answer. There is also the issue about what if the electronic media are being used to purvey completely illegal or criminal activity, to launder drug money or to pirate pieces of creative material, especially for example, from the music industry.

Now there's an argument that developed last year in the United States arguing that there should be what was known as a clipper chip, that in every piece of material where it is encrypted, being passed in scrambled fashion, that the authorities should be able to intervene on any piece of information and unscramble it at will. I don't accept that because the implications for civil liberties and, indeed, the implications for commercial confidentiality are overwhelming. So how then do you ensure that national authorities do have the ability to de-encrypt where it is clearly necessary for them to do so, where criminal activity is being undertaken? My answer would be to apply the search warrant principle that at the moment we use for searching someone's house. If you get special judicial authority for a specific reason in order to search someone's property, why don't we apply exactly the same principle in order to seek de-encryption of material on the electronic networks.

These are a few thoughts about some of the issues that are thrown up by this difficult area of expression and censorship. I believe, to come back to the start, that we have to hold fast to a number of fairly fundamental principles about the importance of free expression, about the need for some limits, but very carefully defined limits. Only with the greatest of circumspection applied, we need to ensure that as far as the electronic media are concerned, we are applying precisely the same principles as we do in any other form of communication, because that is the only fair basis on which to approach it. We also need to recognise that there will always be mistakes, that there is no perfect answer to the difficulties in this field. The process of trimming the boundaries of free expression in the interests of society as a whole, is necessarily an imperfect process. It doesn't mean it should be eschewed entirely, but it does mean that it should be tackled with a great deal of care and caution.

Other publications from IPPR's Media and Communications Project

Convergence and the New Media: a Roadmap
Justin Jameson
December 1995 1 86030 019 7 £4.95
Explains the current position of the on-line and broadcast media (with a comprehensive glossary), their effect on society and a possible regulatory framework once the technology is in place.

Policy for the Press
James Curran
November 1995 1 86030 018 9 £4.95
Calls for an integrated programme of media policy and regulation to replace the current order. Proposals include anti-monopoly controls, greater independencies for journalists, help for new ventures from a Media Enterprise Board and a stronger Press Complaints Commission.

New Issues in Universal Service Obligation
Cristina Murroni and Richard Collins
October 1995 1 86030 010 3 £4.95
Poverty is the main reason for being off the telephone network and only schemes designed for the specific needs of low income users can successfully increase penetration rates among the needy. The authors propose that in time the universal service obligation should be extended to other telephone services.

Managing the Information Society
edited by Richard Collins and James Purnell
July 1995 1 86030 003 0 £7.50
A collection of papers on the future of new technologies, where they can lead and how they should be managed.

The Future of the BBC: Commerce, consumers and governance
Richard Collins and James Purnell
February 1995 1 872452 97 3 £4.95
The BBC is one of the country's largest public services, should it face the same degree of reform that other public services have undergone?

A subscription for all the reports from the Media and Communications Services is available from IPPR, priced £30.

Please call Joanne Bailey at IPPR for more details: 0171 470 6100, or write to IPPR, 30–32 Southampton Street, London WC2E 7RA.

EEK LOAN
XB 2568784 0